Rocks

words by Josephine Croser
photographs and illustrations by Lisa James

Contents

Introduction

Earth is a rocky planet.

In this book you can find out about some of Earth's rocks and learn how they are made.

You will also find out how to start a rock collection.

Earth Chart

This chart compares Earth with a peach.

	Peach	Earth
They both have a skin on the outside.	It is called peach skin.	It is called the **crust**. It is rocky.
They both have a hard part in the middle.	It is called the peach pit.	It is called the **core**. It is very hot.
They both have an in-between part.	We eat this. It is called the flesh.	It is called **magma** It is very hot. It moves like thick honey.

Peach

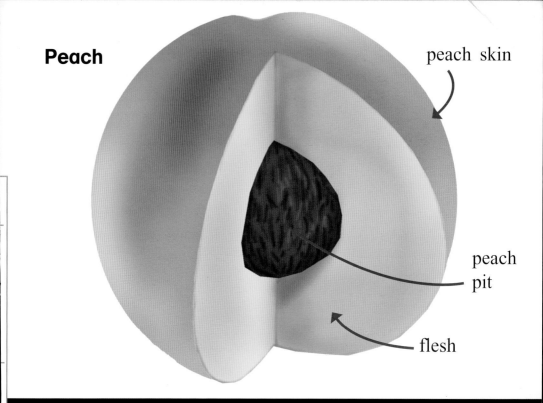

peach skin

peach pit

flesh

Earth

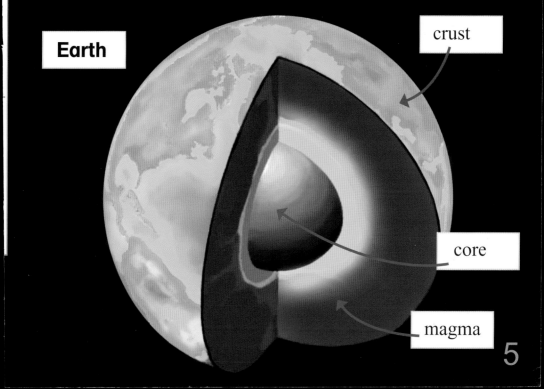

crust

core

magma

5

Rocks from Magma

Sometimes Earth's crust cracks, and hot magma comes out. The magma is then called **lava**, and the crack in the crust is called a **volcano**. When the lava cools, it sets hard. Some lava has bubbles in it, and this lava sets into rocks such as pumice stone. Other rocks have sparkling crystals in them.

Granite

Pumice

Sand and Soil

Rocks do not stay the same forever. Big rocks can break down into small rocks and stones.

The smaller bits of rock break down to become the sand of our beaches and deserts.

Sandstone

Soil

Tiny bits of rock mixed with dead plants and animals make soil. When soil is very wet, it becomes mud. When it is very dry, it can blow around as dust.

Rocks, sand, and soil are all part of Earth's crust.

New Rocks from Old

Many rocks are made when tiny bits
of sand or mud are pressed together
very hard. Often this pressing happens
beneath the sea. Over many, many years,
the bits of sand and mud join together
and become hard. They make new rocks.

Often these rocks have spots or stripes.
The spots were once tiny pebbles or
stones. The stripes were once different
layers of sand or mud.

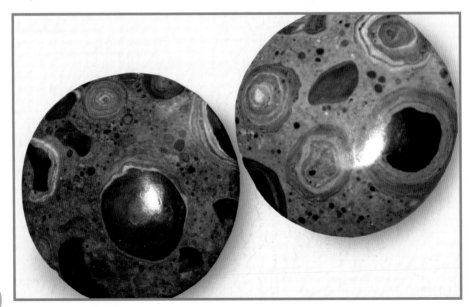

Fossils

Rocks made from sand or mud often have hardened plant or animal bodies inside. These are called **fossils**. Fossils show us plants and animals that lived long ago.

This rock was cracked open. The shell of an animal was inside. It had been hidden there for millions of years.

Sometimes dead trees turn to stone. This rock is a slice of tree trunk. The tree was alive when dinosaurs lived. Now it is a fossil.

Changing Rocks

Rocks change. Wind and water can change them. Water makes rocks smooth. Sand that is blown by the wind can make them rough.

Rock shaped by wind and sand

Heat from magma changes rocks, too. It can make some rocks very hard. It can make crystals grow. This rock has crystals of garnet, a stone used to make jewelry.

Garnet

Space Rocks

Some rocks come to Earth from outer space. As they come through the air, they become very hot and start to melt.

Hot drops of rock and dirt can splash up when a big space rock lands.

The drops then fall down. They cool and set hard.

pie-shaped tektite

meteorites

Collecting Rocks

Collecting rocks is fun and interesting. But remember, you must not take rocks from parks, and you should ask if you can take them from people's land. You need only one sample of each kind of rock you find.

Wash the rocks or brush them with a toothbrush to clean them. Use a magnifying glass to examine each rock carefully. Use the label on page 22 to help you identify each rock in your collection. When you are done, store your rocks in shoeboxes or in a plastic set of drawers.

Label each of your rocks. The label should show these things:

Rock number _____

Name of rock (if you can find out) .

_____

Where it was found _____

When it was found _____

Who found it _____

What it is like _____

_____

(What color is it? Does it sparkle? Is it smooth or rough? Does it have stripes, spots, or fossils?)

We live and walk on a rocky planet. Look for interesting rocks wherever you go.

4. 3. 2. 1.

Index/Glossary

Index

Glossary

pumice Pumice stone comes from lava with bubbles of gas in it. When the lava sets into stone, the bubbles become holes. Pumice stone feels light and rough. Some people buy it and scrub their elbows and heels with it to make them smooth.

space rocks Space rocks are rocks from outer space. If they land on Earth, they are called "meteorites" (MEE-tee-uh-rites). Meteorites can be small, like marbles, or big enough to make a huge hole in the ground.